OREGON COAST

Photography by Steve Terrill
With Selected Prose & Poetry

Oregon Littlebooks

Westcliffe Publishers, Inc.
Englewood, Colorado

First frontispiece: Foxglove in bloom, Cascade Head, Tillamook County
Second frontispiece: Sunset, Cape Meares, Tillamook County
Third frontispiece: Sand dunes, Oregon Dunes National Recreation Area, Lane County
Opposite: Heceta Head Lighthouse, Lane County

International Standard Book Number: 1-56579-120-7
Library of Congress Catalog Number: 94-62088
Copyright Steve Terrill, 1995. All rights reserved.
Published by Westcliffe Publishers, Inc.
2650 South Zuni Street, Englewood, Colorado 80110
Publisher, John Fielder; Editor, Suzanne Venino; Designer, Michelle R. Reeh
Printed in Hong Kong by Palace Press

PREFACE

Thunderous breakers exploding against rocky cliffs...gentle waves rolling across white sand beaches...rugged shores strewn with driftwood...tide pools filled with a kaleidoscope of colors, from vivid orange sea stars and green anemones to ebony muscles and purple sea urchins. The Oregon coast provides visual richness for native Oregonians and visitors alike.

The coastline of Oregon not only has incredible scenic beauty, but it also boasts a colorful history. As I wander around Fort Stevens near the northern tip of Oregon, I think of the events that once transpired here. During World War II this was the only part of the U.S. mainland shelled by a Japanese submarine. Not far from Fort Stevens is Fort Clatsop, where the Lewis and Clark expedition stayed throughout the winter of 1805-06. Today it is a national memorial honoring the explorers.

The coast and the coastal mountains hold a number of national and world records. Near the town of Seaside grows the largest Sitka spruce in the United States, and in the mountains along the coast of Coos County you can find the largest Douglas fir in the country. At the opposite end of the spectrum, the Oregon coast is also renown for smaller records. The "D" River in Lincoln City is known as the world's shortest river, flowing just a brief 440 feet from Devil's Lake to the Pacific Ocean. Depoe Bay lays claim to being the world's smallest harbor.

If breathtaking scenery, history, or world records don't pique your interest, then maybe just simple down-home charm will. Delightful homes and storefront businesses line the boardwalk in Seaside, the longest in the state. Here, the salty sea breezes mingle with the aroma of cotton candy, and, as you stroll along the

Starfish exposed by the receding tide, Cannon Beach, Clatsop County

boardwalk, you may be tempted to stop for a hot dog or a snow cone, reliving happy childhood memories of going to the beach.

More adventurous types can hike the many miles of sand dunes that sweep the shoreline between Florence and North Bend. Hiking these dunes is strenuous, but the rewards are plentiful. You might happen upon one of any number of lakes here, calm pools blanketed with water lilies, as if an oasis in the desert. You may even be lucky enough to see a deer or perhaps a nesting osprey.

My favorite place for hiking and photographing is along the southern stretch of coast between Bandon and Brookings. Not to discredit the central and northern shores, for they, too, are incredibly photogenic, but the southern beaches offer more solitude. Cast among the sea stacks, cliffs, and rock formations are secluded beaches and coves, private places where you can find unexpected treasures — highly prized Japanese glass floats, multi-colored agates, or undisturbed tide pools filled with a profusion of life and color.

To me the Oregon coast is a place I will return to again and again, always to discover something different, to see the landscape in a new light. The images portrayed in this book show just a small part of the drama and beauty to be found along the Oregon coast. I hope these photographs will move you, and perhaps even inspire you to visit our coastline, for there is a part of the Oregon coast for everyone.

— Steve Terrill
Portland, Oregon

Cow parsnip, Neahkahnie Mountain, Tillamook County

"To the attentive eye, each moment of the year has
its own beauty...it beholds, every hour, a picture
which was never seen before,
and which shall never be seen again."
— Ralph Waldo Emerson, Beauty

Fog-shrouded shore,
Cove Beach, Clatsop County

"We do not receive wisdom, we have to discover it
for ourselves by a voyage that no one can take for us..."
— Marcel Proust, Remembrance of Things Past

Yaquina Bay Bridge,
Newport, Lincoln

"Over all, rocks, wood, and water,
brooded the spirit of repose,
and the silent energy of nature
stirred to the soul to its inmost depths."
— Thomas Cole, Essay on American Scenery

Weathered tree stump,
near Arch Cape, Clatsop County

"Great wide, beautiful, wonderful world,
With the wonderful waters round you curled,
And the wonderful grass upon your breast,
World, you are beautifully drest."
— William Brighty Rands, The Child's World

Seaweed-covered sandstone,
Seal Rock State Wayside, Lincoln County

"What is harder than rock, or softer than water?
Yet soft water hollows out hard rock. Persevere."
— Ovid, Ars Amatoria

Patterned sandstone,
Seal Rock State Wayside, Lincoln County

Overleaf: Sea stacks, south of Indian Beach, Clatsop County

"The thunder of the water-wall
Fills the chasm with its fall . . .
And I see the high-hung watery dome
Breaking in a feathery comb
Of foam . . ."
— Friedrich Adler, By the Waterfall

Youngs River Falls,
Clatsop County

"...a taste for the beautiful is most cultivated out of doors..."
— Henry David Thoreau, Walden

Two of the "Three Graces,"
near Garibaldi, Tillamook County

"What would the world be, once bereft
Of wet and of wildness? Let them be left,
O let them be left, wildness and wet;
Long live the weeds and the wilderness yet."
— Gerard Manley Hopkins, Inversnaid

Bloodstar in tidal pool,
Depoe Bay, Lincoln County

"Everybody needs beauty...places to play in
and pray in where Nature may heal and cheer
and give strength to the body and soul alike."
— John Muir, Travels in Alaska

Arch Rock,
Samuel H. Boardman State Park, Curry County

"We are as near to heaven by sea as by land."
— Humphrey Gilbert, A Book of Anecdotes

Cannon Beach coastline,
from Ecola State Park, Clatsop County

"And forget not that the earth delights to feel
your bare feet and
the winds long to play with your hair."
— Kahlil Gibran, The Prophet

Dune patterns,
Pistol River State Park, Curry County

"Someone must be
unstringing them wildly —
white beads shower down
without pause . . ."
— Ariwara No Narihira, On Nunobiki Waterfall

Munson Creek Falls,
highest waterfall in the Coast Range, Tillamook County

Overleaf: Lupine in bloom, Lone Ranch Beach, Curry County

"Come forth into the light of things,
Let Nature be your Teacher."
—William Wordsworth, The Tables Turned

Early morning fog,
Indian Beach, Ecola State Park, Clatsop County

"The visible marks of extraordinary... power appears so plainly
in all the works of creation
that a rational creature who will but
seriously reflect on them
cannot miss the discovery of a deity."
—John Locke, An Essay Concerning Human Understanding

Spouting Horn,
Depoe Bay, Lincoln County

"Everyday life is a stimulating mixture of order and haphazardry.
The sun rises and sets on schedule
but the wind bloweth where it listeth."
— Robert Louis Stevenson, Pan's Pipes

Lincoln City Kite Festival,
Lincoln County

"How often we forget all time, when lone
Admiring Nature's universal throne
Her woods, her wilds, her waters intense
Reply of hers to our intelligence."
— Lord Byron, The Island

View of the coastline from Cape Kiwanda,
Tillamook County

"Solitude . . . is essential to any depth of meditation or of character; and solitude in the presence of natural beauty and grandeur, is the cradle of thoughts and aspirations . . ."
— John Stuart Mill, Principles of Political Economy

The Devil's Punchbowl,
Devil's Punchbowl State Park, Lincoln County

"To him who in the love of Nature holds
Communion with her visible forms, she speaks
A various language."
— William Cullen Bryant, Thanatopsis

Green anemone in tidal pool,
Depoe Bay, Lincoln County

"Little drops of water, little grains of sand,
Make the mighty ocean, and the pleasant land,
So the little moments, humble though they be,
Make the mighty ages of eternity."
— Julia Carney, Little Things

Secluded cove,
Samuel H. Boardman State Park, Curry County

Overleaf: Wind-blown dunes along Heceta Beach, near Florence, Lane County

"Let us permit nature to have her way:
she understands her business better than we do."
— Montaigne, Essays III

Solitary sea stack,
Cape Blanco State Park, Curry County

"There is a road from the eye to the heart
that does not go through the intellect."
— G. K. Chesterton, The Defendant

Hillside of foxglove,
near Astoria, Clatsop County

"The voice of the sea speaks to the soul.
The touch of the sea is sensuous,
enfolding the body in its soft, close embrace."
— Kate Chopin, The Awakening

Fishing boat passing Coquille River Lighthouse,
Coos County

"The noblest of the elements is water."
— Pindar, Olympian Odes

Rugged coastline along Samuel H. Boardman State Park,
Curry County

Wave-washed rocks, near Seaside, Clatsop County